# So, What's Grief Really Like?

*a book about grief and loss*

Susan-Rose McIntyre

Copyright © 2025 Susan-Rose McIntyre

Published in 2025 by Fairlawne Publishing

All rights reserved.

No part of this book may be used or reproduced, distributed, or transmitted in any form or by any means, including photocopying, recording, or other electronic or mechanical methods, without the proper written permission of the author and publisher, except in the case of brief quotations apart, embodied in critical reviews and other specific non-commercial uses permitted by copyright law. Use of this publication is permitted solely for personal use and must include full attribution of the material's source.

# Testimonials

"This grief help book offers guideposts on the grief journey in the form of reflections and images of some of the experiences encountered. Each reflection captures a feature of the painful process of accepting loss. These descriptions help make sense of grief experiences and hold out the hope that they will lead, in time, to a capacity to live with the loss. It is clear these guideposts have been written by someone who has gone on the grief journey. Susan-Rose McIntyre offers comfort and guidance to those on the painful path of grief - one that cannot be avoided. She has provided a valuable contribution to understanding how we can make sense of grief - which seems to be lacking when we are in the middle of it."

**Dr. Rob Gordon, PhD, FAPS - clinical psychologist, trauma specialist**

"This is a delightful book with powerful images and reflections of grief. The stories point to unconscious processes that inform the grief journey. The stories are gentle, reflective, and wise. They point to the wisdom and growth that can be found after loss without skipping over the harshness and pain of grieving."

**Dr. Annie Cantwell-Bartl, PhD, FAPS - psychologist and bereavement specialist**

"So, What's Grief Really Like? gives us descriptions that will resonate with the grief experiences of many and provides a valuable contribution to a deeper understanding of grief. The tasks and gentle tips that arise from these descriptions, informed by prevailing grief theories, will be particularly valuable for grievers."

**Dr. Martin Ryan, PhD - bereavement specialist**

# DEDICATION

*To all those who have loved,*
*and now grieve.*

# Contents

**Introduction 1**

**Part One: The Requisition 7**
Ride The Wild Mustang 9

**Part Two: Reacting & Responding 13**
Paradoxical Grief 15
Ginger in the Stir-Fry 17
One Silver Flute…and more 21
And Then There Were Two 25
The Lounge Room Invasion 29
The Runaway Man 35
The Garden Pond 37
The Patchwork Quilt 43
The Under Water Trick 49
The Shedding Begins 53
Tending the Wound 59
The Grief Twister 63

**Part Three: Reflecting & Recreating 67**
The Waiting Room 69
The Gold Panners 75
The Heart Strings 81
Rowing to the Isle of Loss 89

The Lava Pool 93
The Cloak of Feathers 97
Caught in a Rip 101
The Grotto Within 107

**Part Four: Reacquainting & Renewal 113**

The Stray Cat 115
My Personal Pyramid 121
Pebble in the Shoe 125
Release of the Dove 131
The Invisible Backpack 137
The Pearl Diver 143
The Tapestry Weaver 147
Metamorphosis 153

**Acknowledgements 159**

*We, the fragmented,*
*wake each morning*
*to a kaleidoscopic world.*

*Through ever-changing lenses*
*we are impelled to view,*
*and yet the light shines through.*

DEAR FELLOW TRAVELER,
As you begin your grief journey, I want to reassure you that you do not travel this journey alone.

You belong to a community of grievers, those who have traversed the terrain of grief before, the rough and the smooth of it - and there are many of them. Being part of 'this grief thing' may be all too new for you. As the experience of grief is not often openly shared, we can be surprised to discover just how many members of this hidden community there truly are.

I am also a member of the community of grievers. I began my grief journey over a decade ago with the unexpected death of my only child and son, a beautiful young man, loved by many. I had known losses before and had grieved for them. Still, the magnitude of losing him was like rolling all my past losses together and multiplying them by one hundred. I was left wondering how I would take my next step, uncertain if I would ever be able to stand tall and live life fully again.

*As the days, months, and years of my grief journey passed, I began observing myself in my grief, witnessing with some degree of objectivity how I was responding to this tragedy. I noticed my emotional ups and downs, the changing interactions with others, and the alteration of my once rock-solid beliefs, which were now being truly scrutinized and re-prioritized. One thing became very clear - grief kept changing its form. It was kaleidoscopic in nature - unique, unpredictable, and ever-changing. During my reflections, analogies came to me often. I used these to describe elements of my grief to others who were trying to understand what I was going through. They 'got it.' It appeared that this form of language could 'cut through' and articulate well the seemingly inexplicable.*

*I began to make a collection of these analogies, writing them in an extended narrative form. They explained well 'the blues and the golds' revealed to me as my personal grief exploration unfolded. I was encouraged to share many of these - hard-won as they were. My desire in writing this collection is that others negotiating their own grief path may be assisted in finding some clarity themselves - 'a way through.'*

## So, What's Grief Really Like?

*A recommendation in reading this book is that it not be read in one sitting. Instead, each chosen analogy, selected for its appropriateness at the time, be read in isolation. A reflection time to follow each reading would be helpful - a time for personal processing. It might be that a particular analogy may 'bring something to the surface' for you. You may wish to share this with others, or write about it in a journal, or reflect upon it yourself in your own time - in your own way.*

*There are brief, gentle tips and suggested grief work tasks at the end of each reflection. These are provided by way of assisting with the process of practically transferring key themes into one's day-to-day living. These, of course, are optional for the reader - nothing at all about grieving is compulsory. Grief is as individual and unique to each person as their fingerprint.*

*There is a strong message running throughout the book stressing the importance of self-care - it is so tough at times, as we all know. We need to listen to ourselves and be willing to seek out that which we truly need at different times.*

*As you peruse the book, feel free to select randomly, choosing those pieces that appear to be a match for you at the time - the kaleidoscope of grief is forever changing.*

*Be kind to yourself as you begin, and pace yourself as you move through. Many stories touch upon raw emotions that are all part of the mix of grief. Take in only as much as you wish and feel you are ready for.*

*Go gently,*

*Susan-Rose*

# Introduction

## Grief - what is it?

IT CAN BE DEFINED AS a response to loss, manifesting in the commencement of an inner personal process that encompasses the physical, psychological, emotional, and possibly the spiritual aspects of ourselves.

The loss involved may take many forms: the death of a loved one, the loss of an identity, a place, a relationship, an animal or object, employment, loss of potential, loss of a dream, loss through disability or a tragic accident - the list goes on. Grief experiences, we know, can be mild or profound. Overall, acknowledgement and social discussion around grief do not often occur, leaving most of us uncertain how to respond to someone in grief. This, of course, is until we find that it is we, ourselves, who are immersed in it - left feeling alone, fearful, and ignorant. It is only then that we find ourselves compelled to find ways to face it and negotiate 'a path through.'

Grief is a moving feast from which we must all eventually partake. It can present in many different guises, and as such, analogies can be an ideal way to reveal something of its changeable nature. They provide us with an accessible language for grief, a process that can be both difficult to grasp and articulate. In this collection, I have tried to reveal something of my own grief journey after the loss of my only child, as well as insights gained from descriptions heard from fellow grievers, in the hope others connect with these. I hope, too, that these analogies for grief may provide some clarity and 'hooks for understanding' which may assist in making some sense of this crazy, confusing, chaotic ride we find ourselves having to undertake.

Primarily, grief is an individual process. It is not linear, sequential, or cyclical. It takes each of us on a unique self-made trail, with no compass or map. We discover there is no right way to grieve - we learn as we go; each finding our own way, our own methods. It can be a journey full of surprises. It can pull us up in the middle of our tracks or present us with ever-changing views. Grief's power can strip us to our core, leaving us with the daunting task of rebuilding - at times, a seemingly impossible task. A thread of hope and faith in our own ability to 'get through' may be all that we have in finding the courage to begin. Fortunately, as many have testified, this can be enough. In the darkness, we each find our own light, our own rocks in the storms, our own style of grieving, to eventually manage our loss.

As it happens, my descriptions, intuitively arrived at after long periods of personal reflection, mirror well many of the latest recognized academic theories and models for the grief process.

While studying for a Master's degree in Counseling, specializing in bereavement counseling, it was gratifying to learn that my personal theories had some evidence-based credibility. Many of my analogies depict common elements of the grieving process. These encompass various themes, including integration, adaptation, self-care, managing emotions, styles of grieving, vacillation, and the multifaceted nature of the grief process.

Following each reflection outlined in the book, you will find some 'grief tasks' clarifying various aspects of grief work, and some 'gentle tips' to assist with this.

Though grief is not an experience we may willingly wish to undertake, we come to realize, however, there is often little choice in the matter - loss is part of life. Grief's importance and influence as a healthy and honorable response to loss need to be acknowledged and more fully recognized. Sadly, death and grief, particularly in Western culture, remain among the last taboo subjects for open discussion. I hope that this book will assist in some way to dispel the many myths, fears, and stigma surrounding death and grief so that they begin to receive the respect and dignity deserved. These 'landmark points in our lives' need to be recognized as the profound experiences they truly are.

The grievers, and in fact, all of us, would certainly be the richer for it.

# PART ONE

## THE REQUISITION

# RIDE THE WILD MUSTANG

I AM THE WILD, SILVER MUSTANG you may only have glimpsed in the past, or perhaps had only heard of through tales of dread whispered by others summoned before. I roam free and untethered in distant hills, but now encircle you.

I am here, daring you to heed me, lift your head, and stare directly into my cobalt blue eyes, eyes that can pierce deep down into your soul, where your truth lies. I want you to greet me full on. Give it over to me, surrender. You have not needed me before, but now I make my presence felt. I stamp my hoof, strong and resonant, demanding that you reveal yourself and step forward.

I can frighten, torment, persist, keep you awake at night, until you respond. I challenge you to mount me, cling to my mane, and take the ride. You will be transported to places never previously imagined. To mysterious, damp and dark hollows, thick with ferns dripping with the night's rain; mountain peaks too, snow-tipped and sublime in their beauty with panoramic views - views of marvel and wonder. This journey may indeed be treacherous. It will not be without its risks. My pace will be ever-changing, at times a furious gallop, then calming to a slow, rhythmic trot. I will never allow you to be completely still. A moody, unpredictable beast, I live only for my own expression, but this can mean yours, too.

You cannot bridle me but must allow me to roam free. I will permit you, though, to come close when your trust has grown. Let you stroke me and whisper in my ear as we ride, question me. We can share our truths as we go. Let me gallop and have my head when you feel you have the strength. You will learn to connect with me and how to appease me when my pace overwhelms, being all too much. Slowly, you will come to know me, my nature, my ways. We will tune into each other and eventually get the rhythm right; learn to move as one.

Take heed, I warn you now, never try to shut me out, and walk away before we are done, for I will kick and kick and gnaw at the stable door until you lift the latch. I have a constant urge to be set free to whinny as loud as I please, jump impossibly high fences, wander as I desire. Yours is a compulsory ride; I will that you take it, lest you remain engulfed by regret and riddled with fear.

Come, jump the hurdles with me: walls of stone, bracken, and brambles. We can clear them with room to spare. I will teach you to face them all; nothing can stand in our way. And when our ride is done, and we are honestly spent, you will be returned to dismount and rejoin the folk who have been waiting for you.

But always remember when you hear my heavy hoof's deep pounding on the earth in the distance, in the depths of the night or the starkness of the day, just whistle, soft and light, and I will return to carry you away. For this is how I will always remind you, and never let you forget the depths of the love you once shared.

> **Task:** To meet and accept the challenge of facing your grief and letting go of your fear of it. Be willing to 'go with it' and discover what revelations and restorations your individual grief journey can bring.

*Gentle Tip: Be open and creative with your grief. Personalize its expression so that it becomes truly authentic and meaningful for you.*

# Part Two

## Reacting & Responding

# Paradoxical Grief

Grief

a paradox,

able to weaken and strengthen,

tenderly embrace or ensnare with the force of an

eagle's claw

~ We are left bewildered.

Grief

a change-master,

wielding a power to perplex,

to bring out the best in us, and the worst.

To lord over us or humbly serve our needs,

gently massaging a soothing balm into weary limbs,

or thumping with a club so hard

~ We fall to our knees.

Grief

so oftentimes feared,

is hushed and hidden away,

it threatens to unveil us,

layer by layer,

stripping us to our core,

revealing to all

~ Who we really are.


Grief

a paradox,

an unwanted gift, wrapped in black,

one barely acknowledged,

very quickly shelved;

Quite simply, too risky, too capricious.

~ We are left in fear.

# Ginger in the Stir-Fry

THE FIRST TIME I TASTED ginger, it was foreign and overpowering. It dominated all the other flavors, no matter how rich or how many.

I would prepare my favorite dishes, perhaps a risotto or a pear crumble, only to discover they had been laced with ginger. Repulsed, it was all I could do not to spit out each mouthful, though, oftentimes, I did. I resented so much ginger's ability to drown out and distort all the other delicious flavors I knew and loved. I vowed I would rather not have meals at all if they had to come with ginger.

Friends and family tried earnestly to change my view, pleading that ginger was a worthy ingredient, adding so much, 'that special tang.' It provided some balance to an otherwise incomplete dish. They claimed, too, that it had a cleansing, healing quality, somewhat medicinal in nature.

Whenever I visited my Aunt Jennifer, she would offer me a mug of ginger tea.

"So soothing," she'd declare. "It reaches deep inside, to the very corners of you, love." She swore it had healed all her wounds. Believing so much in the benefits of this humble root, she made a point of having a slice or two each day. She promised it would do me the world of good if only I would be more accepting, less resistant.

On a cool afternoon, during one of my visits to her house, we sat across from each other at her kitchen table. Aunt Jen offered me a sip from her mug of warm ginger tea. I had been quietly watching her drink it as she spoke, and with each sip she seemed to 'gain something,' hard to describe, but there was definitely a change. With each mouthful, she seemed to become more settled, more at peace, truer to herself. Her whole being seemed steadier, calmer, more assured. Her clear, blue eyes twinkled a little as she pushed her mug toward me, coaxing me to try it; give it a go.

"Dare I?" I asked myself.

Tentatively, I lifted the mug to my lips. The distinctive aroma filled my nostrils, its 'gingerliness' was all-pervading. I felt woozy, a little sick inside. "Be brave," I told myself. I took a sip and was surprised - I was not repulsed after all. It was not as bitter as expected. Aunt Jen urged me to have some more. I took a second gulp, then another. I felt this warm foreign brew trickle down, caressing my raspy parched throat. I felt it filter through my entire system, bathing it, soothing it, balm-like.

"More love, have it all. Let it work on you," she gently urged. Sip by sip, I drank it all down, letting it in, letting it integrate. Something began to stir deep inside. With each mouthful, I felt its healing powers begin to work on me, on my woes held deep within - my unacknowledged aches, my secret pains were starting to surface. The distortions, the twisted kinks of my punishing thinking, were finally beginning to unravel. Tears welled up. I had held them down for so long; my well's lid had been lifted. I started to feel true to myself. It had been a long time.

"That's the way, love. Let it in so you can let it out." Aunt Jennifer smiled across the table to me, nodding as she spoke, "That's the way. It gets a little easier with every sip."

**Task:** To acknowledge your hurts, your grief pains, so that the healing can begin. Learning to integrate grief into a new way of being and being true to your emotions.

***Gentle Tip:*** *Start slow, with small portions to begin. Bit by bit, let grief in to work on you. You may well find your capacity to swallow a little more each day increases so that you begin to appreciate and benefit from its restorative qualities. Express your sorrow as you choose. Grief is its own medicine.*

# ONE SILVER FLUTE...AND MORE

I REACHED FOR MY SILVER FLUTE, my constant companion of late. It could sing for me; sing up raw feelings from the very depths of me. I could breathe fully into it, synchronize with it; my breath bringing it to life and it giving life to my breath, my essence. It was able to reach deep down into my soul, drawing up the sorrows and the joys. My flute held the wondrous power of releasing my cage of hushed and hooded birds trapped within. Its pure notes able to loosen the cage's latch, allowing my captives to soar; to free-lark and encircle me, finally able to fly free. Its notes, pure and true, allowing all barriers to fall away. No disguises, no muffled notes, no untruths - just simple, pure expression. I would become at one with my instrument - so grateful for it in my grief.

But what has happened? My pure golden notes can no longer be heard. They're now drowned out; smothered. Was that a tuba? A pair of clashing cymbals? Some deafening drums? An organ? Surely not. How could this be when it is the flute alone I hold to my lips? My flute's tune had become unrecognizable to me; every note now overlaid with a tirade of foreign ones - loud and imposing. My flute's entire melody was now horribly amplified and distorted - all was in discord. It was as if I had become a one-man band compelled to play a host of instruments all at the same time.

Friends around me covered their ears, ran to hide. They lost trust in me, never knowing what I would come out with next. My head was filled with a din, a disturbing cacophony. Fear began to rise. Flute playing completely lost its appeal. How this had come about was beyond me to explain.

I longed for the return of some simplicity, some clarity, some peace.

> **Task:** To examine whether there is a possibility that there are some past losses that you have not fully acknowledged and expressed. Is there a chance that a past loss may have become entangled in your current grief, clouding and complicating it?

*Gentle Tip*: *Observe yourself in your grieving. If you find that your emotions are 'over the top' or seemingly inappropriate for your current loss experience, it may be worth examining whether a past loss, which has been lying dormant, is being triggered by your current loss. If this is the case, your grief experience may have become clouded, amplified, and inappropriately strong. Others around you may become confused and not understand some of your reactions. It would be wise to revisit and address some of your past loss experiences. Some guidance may be needed with this to allow yourself to fully discover and express any repressed emotions you may be unknowingly harboring.*

## And Then There Were Two

I WAKE IN THE DARK - you're there.
Shuffle into the light-flooded kitchen to make a hot drink - you're there.

Turn on the TV to catch a few minutes of a movie rerun. Hear your mutterings on my shoulder, can't follow the plot - cursing you, I flip the switch; give up.

Back in bed, your relentless diatribe starts up. You keep on, always trying to dump your stuff on me. I toss and turn, turn and toss, trying to escape its fall.

Come morning, I feel like a mound of wet sand; sodden, dense, immovable. At the bathroom basin, shaving for work, you're there, watching me - I cut myself.

Speeding down the freeway, foot heavy on the pedal, I sense you in the car - a jabbering raven pecking at me, incessantly.

At my work station, trying to type, you constantly interrupt, interrogate with your double-checking, with your insatiable desire for finer and finer details.

"Tell me what happened again, how come he died? Why couldn't you stop it?"

For a break, I go out for lunch with some of the boys - you come too, so what's new?

They don't get it - my pre-occupation, and neither do I.

Fed up, I decide to challenge, confront you, face you full on, "Butt out! Just clear off. This hounding has to stop. Your grip is suffocating. It's over, I'm done with you!"

I shuffle back to the office, a sense of victory daring to creep in. But then, a quiet chattering, that familiar monologue starts up, "Tell me how come he died again?"

Clearly, you are not done with me.

**Task:** To come to terms with the 'ongoing nature' of the grief process. To give yourself time and space to devote to your grieving, but also to find ways to have some control over it so that grieving doesn't dominate to such an extent that you find it difficult to function.

*Gentle Tip: At first, we may seem to be thinking about our loss and consumed by grief all the time. Given time, and with our own processing, periods of reprieve begin to appear. We eventually find that we can fully enter into some activities without grief always being present. We aim to find ways to compartmentalize and manage our grieving time, making life more manageable.*

# THE LOUNGE ROOM INVASION

ONE MINUTE I AM SITTING on my favorite couch, thumbing through a magazine, and the next I am being completely engulfed by something, something truly horrific and unrecognizable. Some kind of dark monster was unfolding and expanding in the middle of my lounge room, encroaching on me on all sides. I was being completely smothered by it, barely able to breathe.

Frozen with shock, I could only bear witness as it swelled and invaded every corner of the room and every one of my senses. The smell of rubber, sickening and strong, filled my nostrils with every one of my panicky breaths. The taste of rubber overwhelmed me; I became a prisoner, pinned down and compelled to endure the indignity of being force-fed. I thrashed about in desperation, pleading for it to end. I could hear the air rushing into its form with a hideous hissing sound. It was impossible to assess the size of this thing. So close to it, I was completely overcome by its enormity. I tried to measure its girth with outstretched arms to know something of its shape - without success. This was surely an alien, or perhaps a ravenous beast that had somehow invaded my known world.

This, of course, could only be a horrid dream I was in, one I would surely wake from at any moment. This would never happen. No, it couldn't possibly be real. All would return to normal, and this invader, this ravenous clawing monster, would disappear, just vanish when I woke. Trouble was - I was awake. I thought of trying to get some verification from friends, family members, anyone. Could they see it too? Had the arrival of this thing impacted them? But there was no escaping; they all knew exactly what I was talking about; they had felt it too: the horror, the shock, the chaos. No one would deny its existence, even if I pleaded with them to.

There was nothing for it; with gritted teeth and every ounce of courage I possessed, I stood on unsteady legs and moved towards it. I began to feel my way around it, one step at a time, cautiously, tentatively. I wanted to know what had struck me, what it was. I wanted to know all about it, what it was made of; its texture, its hollows and rises, its nature.

Stepping slowly sideways around its edges, I ran my hands over it, trying to feel something familiar - but nothing. I did this daily, circumnavigating it, examining it closely as I inched my way round, asking myself, "What can it be? Why was it here? Why had I been chosen to have this blast into my life? How was I going to live with this in-your-face invader?"

Waking to its presence day after day, I eventually resigned myself to the fact that even though it was indeed huge and frightening, I knew I would have to find some way to manage it and live with it, as impossible as that seemed.

After much exploration, I was surprised to find that it was slightly malleable and receptive to some of my own pushing and pulling. I could have a hand in shaping it after all. I also discovered that I could park it in different places in my lounge room, allowing me space to continue doing some things as I used to. Some normality was beginning to return. I had a growing sense of unease, however, that things would never, could never, be as they once were.

After a long time spent just sitting with it, examining it from all angles, some objectivity began to appear. Then it struck me. What had actually arrived was, in fact, a large inflatable life raft. It struck me, too, that paradoxically, this precarious craft might well be my salvation. There might be some positivity in this after all. Some opportunities might be on offer here. Perhaps, this craft could carry me to new horizons - horizons I had never before dreamed of reaching.

I knew it wouldn't be easy stepping into it: doubt, nervousness, fear, all coming on board as well. But deep inside, I had a real sense that this was one venture I must accept and undertake. With a bundle of misgivings and with my heart beating double time, I rose from my chair, moved closer, and stepped on board.

Steadying myself, I sat down on the small rubber seat and reached for the oar.

> **Task:** To recover from the shock of your loss and learn to face and accept the reality of it. To explore grief's nature and its influence. To lessen your fear of it.

***Gentle Tip:*** *Take time to get to know the nature of your grief. Accept support in your recovery from trusted others. If you can, use your grief in a positive way to keep you afloat. Use its energy to honor your loved one in your own unique way. Be prepared to reassess your life goals and make changes. Allow for movement in a different direction* *if that seems right for you. There may be an opportunity for post-traumatic growth to eventuate.*

# The Runaway Man

Run, rush, hide, hurry,
No standing zones,
It'll catch up.
Dart, dash, divert, deflect,
I'm a twister
in a Teflon suit.
Slip, slip, slippery, slip
It won't be able to get a grip.
Change everything, stir it up
Move it, move it - work till I drop.
Run, rush, hurry, scurry
Stir the dust, all's a flurry
It'll never ever catch me, that's for sure.
I've run away from much more before,
Can run away from this too, I can.
Just watch me -
Yeah, you just watch me, man.
Grief 'll never catch me; I have my ways,

I'll outrun this for the rest of my days
'Cause why? you ask.
'Cause I'm the Runaway Man.

**Task:** To be prepared to acknowledge that you are in grief, and to take time to deal with it.

***Gentle Tip:*** *Try as we might, through overworking, staying busy, doing lots of traveling, or finding any diversion (including overusing substances), grief cannot be outrun or smothered. It just waits for us to stop eventually, and acknowledge its presence. At some point, we need to turn, face it, and deal with it.*

# THE GARDEN POND

## Encircling

LUCY AND I WERE TOLD the sad news last week. Now Lucy just goes on and on about it; she won't let it rest. There's nothing good in that. I wish she'd see sense and stop moping about. This will never do. We can only do what we can do, nothing more. Keep the ship running, keep things afloat, I say - that way we won't all fall in a heap.

"Yes, I know what's happened. I've heard the news. You know that I know, Lucy, so why do you want me to talk about it, sit with you, and listen constantly - hold you, rock you. Just let things be. Tears and talk will get us nowhere with all of this. Life goes on, and the jobs don't stop. Have you noticed that pond he and I built together down the back - well, we've let it go; it's surrounded by blackberries. The archer statue has fallen in, and the water pump's broken. It's a disgrace! What would he think if he could see it now? He'd think he didn't matter to us. He'd think we'd forgotten him. I'm going to make it my goal over the next few weeks to restore it to its former glory. If you can't find me, that's where I'll be. I'll have to order a pallet of slate pieces, lay them around the pond, install a new water pump, and remount the archer statue. I remember he bought it for me for Father's Day two years back. Yes, that's what's needed: less talk and more action. Sitting around mulling things over and over, feeling miserable, will get us nowhere; never has, never will. We have to take some control here - action is the answer. Now, where's my tool kit?"

- Jed.

## Immersion

"Jed, he's so cold-hearted. How can he just carry on as though nothing has happened? All he can talk about is fixing that wreck of a pond in our backyard while I sit here in total shock.

My heart aches so much, I can barely move. How can I make him understand how I feel? He's like some kind of crustacean with an impermeable exoskeleton! Just a little emotion, one tear even, would show me that he really does have some softness; does possess a heart. Is that too much to ask at a time like this?

I'm saturated, drenched to the bone. I've been cast into this 'pond of grief,' cold, murky, and deep. I'm entangled in its sinewy weeds, entrapped, enmeshed, and yet feel compelled to stay - to experience it fully. I reach up searching for an answer, some way through. But no, I wade deeper and deeper into it, hoping full immersion will bring some communion with you that I'm certain is bound to occur. I can't be persuaded to rise up, 'Leave it alone for a bit,' as Jed expects of me. Time means nothing to me now. No matter what the urgency, I won't step out of my new watery world. I'm like a mollusc clinging desperately to a rock of hope, wanting to grasp onto you and stay bonded forever in this inky darkness. I want so desperately to connect with you. If I am here with you, I can't possibly have lost you. It is here I curse, howl, and yearn - if only you could return."

- Lucy

> **Task:** To understand that there are different styles of grieving. To allow each griever the freedom to choose to grieve in their own way.

---

*Gentle Tip: For those who are the 'doers' (the 'instrumentals'\*), this does not mean they do not feel; it is just that they cannot outwardly express their emotions and prefer to 'think' and 'act' instead. Commonly, but not always, men tend to grieve in an instrumental style. Others, the 'feelers' (the 'intuitives'\*), display their emotions openly: the hurt, the sorrow, the yearning. It can be difficult for each to comprehend the style of the other's grief, though both are legitimate. Women are often more expressive with their feelings; more intuitive in the way* *they grieve. However, we must remember that gender does not dictate a grieving style preference. The way each of us grieves remains very personal and individual. Much patience and tolerance will be needed to prevent misunderstandings through presumption. Remember, too, that many people grieve with a blend of both styles, combining both practical and emotional elements.*

---

*\*The terms 'intuitive griever' and 'instrumental griever' originate from the grief model theory proposed by Kenneth J. Doka and Terry L. Martin (1999).*

# The Patchwork Quilt

There had been a dreadful storm in the night. I had hung my treasured patchwork quilt on the line for an airing the day before.

The following morning, I spied it through the kitchen window and saw it there on the line - drooping, lifeless, and storm-weary. I cursed myself for forgetting to bring it in. I realized it had endured the terrible onslaught of the night. For hours, it would have been tossed about by wild winds and pelted with harsh, unrelenting rain. How could I have let this happen? What was I thinking? I rushed out to retrieve it, hoping there would be little harm done. By this time, the storm was long gone, and the mid-morning sun had begun spreading its fingers of warmth.

I was shocked to see how my quilt had been so severely affected. I noticed it had dried in a really strange way - once smooth and perfect, it was now almost completely covered in wrinkles; every patch looked like overused crepe paper. With tears in my eyes, I pulled it from the line, and, nursing it across my arms, carried it inside, where I began furiously ironing it.

I ironed and ironed but my frustrations began to rise. It was clear - this was not going to be a simple task. My quilt had been significantly changed and would never, could never, be the same again. I noticed, too, there was something really peculiar about it. Each morning when I examined the quilt, the wrinkles seemed to have shifted to different patches - ones I thought I had already tended to would be wrinkled again. I'd set about, once more, ironing them flat, but those wrinkles would simply resurface in a few days. There seemed to be no logic to it - no method, no cure. The randomness of the wrinkles' appearance was so vexing; my ironing seemed pointless. I didn't seem to be getting anywhere with it. The look and feel of my 'almost ruined' quilt was heartbreaking.

One morning, as I was once again trying to iron out a new day's display of wrinkles, I heard a knock at the back door. It was Isla from next door, my elderly neighbor.

"Come to see how y' gettin' on, love," she sang out, as I opened the back door. Dear Isla was just the person I needed at that moment. In she tottered and, sitting at my kitchen table, began gazing at my quilt spread across it. After studying it carefully, she declared, "Oh, I had a quilt like this one once, dear. A quilt like this seems to have a mind of its own. Have you found that?" I nodded in silence. "See those stubborn crinkly patches, don't worry, you'll see that most of them should clear with time, and a good load of patience. It takes as long as it takes, you know. Can't rush these things. They work their way out in their own time, but you need to give them some attention all the same. Time, patience, plus a bit of elbow grease, that usually does the trick."

I listened, hanging on her every word. It was so good to hear from someone who had not only experienced a blow similar to mine, but from one who had resolved it as well.

"But, don't be surprised either, love, if some of your wrinkles refuse to be smoothed out altogether and never quite vanish - you might just have to wear those, live with them, as they say. I drape my quilt across my bed each night; it warms and comforts me all the same, wrinkles and all. Just don't let it get to you now - that would be my advice to you."

Her words were like a welcome summer breeze, giving me some hope.

I followed Isla's advice and ironed my quilt with patience daily, giving each wrinkly patch a little water spray and a gentle press with a warm iron.

And yes, things did improve, as Isla predicted. With the extra regular gentle care, most of the wrinkles eventually lifted, but, just like her own quilt,

I found that even after what seemed an age, a few wrinkly patches refused to budge - and they are there to this day. Not many folks notice - it is only a few wised-up quilt owners who can usually pick them out.

Thankfully, as time has passed, I've come to accept those stubborn patches. They are part of the make-up of this special, unique quilt of mine.

It is what it is - no other like it.

> **Task:** To acknowledge the uniquely individual nature of your grief. Also, to accept that grief is not a linear, sequential process, but one characterized by randomness and unpredictability.

**Gentle Tip:** *Grief's very nature is unpredictable and ever-changing. It has a randomness that can be hard to deal with. It does not follow a neat sequential movement through a series of stages, as previously thought. We think we have made gains, but can find ourselves back at 'patch* *one' again. Each of us will have our own stubborn 'sticking points' in our individual grief journey - these may need lifelong tending. Strategies such as deep breathing techniques, art therapy or emotional journal keeping may assist. Wise others, such as counselors, or those who have experienced it before, may guide you in the management of resistant grief emotions.*

# The Under Water Trick

I CAN MANAGE. IT'S NOT TOO hard to do. I can do all I have to do: the chores, the shopping, the school run, my job, and the kids. I will surprise you all (and myself) because I can do it all while, wait for it, treading water with a balloon held between my knees. Yes, I'm that clever.

I'm sure nobody would ever guess what I am keeping held down; no hint of it visible. My coping mask I never let slip. I swim about doing all the proper strokes: smiling, laughing, managing small talk, keeping up. All seems just the same - to you. Why is it then that I am so overcome with this terrible weariness?

Why am I so exhausted all the time? The very thought of getting dressed has me diving for the covers. Life's like trying to swim upstream, constantly. You have no idea of the strain I am under, clamping this balloon between my knees while attempting to swim, or even just tread water. Why do I persist in trying to do the impossible when every cell in my body is screaming at me, "We can't do this any longer; it's too hard - Get Real!"

The strain is beginning to show. I start to wonder what would happen if I stopped pushing down this balloon, this cursed bubble of woe, and let it rise to the surface – simply let it go. Dare I reveal what's really been going on? Dare I reveal what's been there all the time? Would I drown in the shame, in the sorrow, in the fear of it? Would I stay afloat? There is only one way to know.

Here goes…1, 2, 3, Let it go! Let it show!

> **Task:** Have the courage to reveal the pain of your grief to others, and to yourself. Authenticity can be a lifebuoy. Acknowledge

and reveal the actual impact of your grief. Be authentic to yourself, and to others.

---

**Gentle Tip:**   *Grief can be expressed in many different ways. Find your own ways that suit.*

*Perhaps begin writing a journal to 'write it out' or share your feelings with a trusted one or two. You may well find it surprisingly easier than holding it in. A sense of relief may result. Slowly reveal some elements of your grief with a broader circle - all in your own time. There are no set time limits - pace yourself.*

---

# The Shedding Begins

A FINE SUMMER DAY. PICNIC MAKERS out and about, lolling under shady broad-leafed trees. Children darting between the trunks - laughing, playing, having fun. Drinks are flowing, and a second course is about to begin. Folks chat freely, holding plates in readiness for more generous helpings. Then, without warning, a powerful, chilling wind blasts through, and with it, arrives instant fall.

All that was just fell away. All became devoid of light, life and color. A mass shedding began. All laughter, now nothing but a hollow echo. All food bland and tasteless. Every tree stripped bare, lashed by this wild 'chill-to-the-bone' wind.

Only a cruel starkness remained in its wake. I looked down and was unrecognizable to myself. Now standing there, a bare-branched tree, dead-looking, broken-limbed, alone.

This shedding continued until I was stripped to my core. What would become of me? Another puff of wind and I was sure to topple; my footing so uncertain and insecure. Diminished to a shell of myself, my aura dimmed almost to zero - my day at the family picnic now nothing but a faint memory, distant and irrelevant. Then, from this 'out-of-season' fall, so sudden and unheralded, a long dormancy period commenced.

'Just keep standing,' became my mantra. 'Just keep drawing in the water, the nutrients, the sunlight, just keep on holding on.' It was all I could do.

From the outside, I looked fine, intact, seemingly steady and functioning. No obvious harm done. But internally, a time of profound inner change was underway.

I began constantly reassessing everything I had been so sure about before. My belief that all had been a 'rock solid reality' now truly shaken. I had always known what season it was, hadn't I? Life had its rhythms, its predictability. Little had I known it could all be turned on its head in an instant.

I mourned the passing of my old self, my old world; everything I knew and loved now shed. The world had become foreign to me; I was an outsider cast in a new landscape. My task now: to find my place in it. My stores of resilience were scant, but were all I had - they'd have to suffice.

To others, not a lot seemed to be happening. On the outside, no signs of change, no moving forward, nothing stirring at all. Perhaps they thought I was bowing down to this vicious onslaught; the sudden shock of it plainly all too much for me. Perhaps they feared I wouldn't survive, thinking this would be my last season - the natural cycle of things having been so severely interrupted. Steeped in the depths of it, I was tempted to think so too.

But then, little hints began to appear signalling there was indeed something left within me to regenerate and grow anew. Small valiant shoots of green, just visible, on my stark, brittle branches, trying to push through. Tiny shoots of hope and life. I raised my limbs in gratitude. Spring would once again return. My faith in a future, my future, reclaimed.

> **Task:** To recover from the numbness and shock of early grief and enter into your period of grieving.

---

***Gentle Tip:*** *Fall is the first season of grief, marked by a shedding of so much: perhaps tears, dreams, hopes, painful emotions, possessions, relationships (as they were), and even body weight. The subsequent moving through the seasons takes as long as it takes. We will each have our personal seasons requiring their own expression. There is no natural order to it. Grief is random by nature. Experience each season fully - the good and the bad. Sometimes all four seasons could arrive in one day. During this time, hope and sheer will may lead you to a sense that*

*So, What's Grief Really Like?*

*you can indeed survive this to live life anew. Find ways to nurture yourself as this extraordinary process unfolds.*

---

# Tending the Wound

## Bandage On

EACH MORNING, MY NEW DAILY routine begins. After inspecting my gaping wound, I reach for a fresh bandage. Round and round I wrap the wound firmly and securely, pinning its edge snugly and seamlessly into the top bandage layer. Then I proceed to dress, always making sure not one hint of my bandage is visible, long-sleeved garments alone to be worn. Once dressed and groomed, I am satisfied. They would have no idea! No one would know what it is I am harboring. I'm now able to function, get things done, get on with the game. But, try as I might, there is one person I cannot fool, and that is myself - I know the pain is still there pricking away relentlessly. Who am I kidding? Every minute, I have a constant reminder: throb, throb, throb. I strive to push the sensations down - to get through, be normal, look right.

"How are you traveling?" fellow workers enquire. "All fine, all's good - coping well." I declare three times a day - when I know I'm so clearly not. By mid-afternoon, my wound begins to pulse unbearably. Exhaustion creeps in. My charade starts taking its toll - the effort to pretend to this degree just too great. I have a desperate need to be home, to find relief. At work day's end, once home, I rush to unwrap my wound - so stifled, so sore. Give it air, tend to it. I gently bathe it, dabbing at its red rawness over and over. And as I do, I wonder if this cursed wound will ever truly heal.

## Bandage Off

As I remove the bandage, I inspect my wound - deep and sore. Pain waves throb through my entire system. Each one is a reminder of the loss I feel. I do what I can to address this gaping wound and assist in its healing: examining it closely, bathing it, soothing it. I feel each sting shoot through me. Through gritted teeth, I keep saying to myself, "Just hang on. This will pass, this will pass."

I flush the wound regularly, removing whatever residue I find embedded there. If I don't, I worry that it might fester - turn foul, refuse to heal. This wound makes constant demands on me, robs me of time, and won't be ignored.

I curse its existence. I have too many other things to be getting on with. But tend to it I must, for I know that only then will I begin to live more fully again.

> **Task:** To make time to grieve and tend your grief wound, but also to allow yourself some 'time out' - to put it aside for a while. Bring other things into focus.

***

*Gentle Tip:* *Tending to your grief does not have to be constant and ongoing. Find ways that suit you to manage your grieving time by compartmentalizing it. This will allow you time to be truly present, to focus on your work, interact well with others, and complete many of the necessary everyday tasks that don't go away. Remember, you are not showing disrespect or disloyalty if you spend time away from grieving. Grief does not have to have all of you.*

# The Grief Twister

Born

of rage

it encircles,

enveloping, engulfing,

Venting its vile curse on all who dare to stand in its

path.

Not blown from the south this one,

but sourced and harbored deep within.

Deafening, crashing,

the howling wind

of grief-fuelled wrath

wakens me each night

Swirling incessantly,

scoffing at the window panes,

so thin, pathetic, fragile.

Spun with threads

of incensed

rage,

surging forward.

Tendrils reach out

to feed a hunger,

ravenous and raw.

I am entrapped, gathered up,

can't hold on,

lost in fury,

flung in all directions at once.

Not knowing which way is up, left or right.

Desperate, familiar hands reach in

trying to rescue me,

pull me out.

"Leave me," I scream to them,

"I need this - it's who I am now."

Feeding off each other,

Twister and I

spin, splice, and spiral,

sweeping through,

red and furious.

We leave in our wake a scene of bleak devastation,

Giving me nothing but pure satisfaction.

*So, What's Grief Really Like?*

Wreckage, carnage, and innocent bystanders left
shaking their heads in disbelief,
inspecting their wounds,
and simply asking,
"Why?"

**Task:** To acknowledge the possibility of anger being present, a common grief emotion. To learn to express it safely and effectively.

---

***Gentle Tip:*** *Strong emotions can affect our behaviors, which in turn can affect our relationships. Steeped in grief, with intense anger and resentment present, we may unintentionally hurt those around us, complicating our grief experience. Find ways to work through these intense emotions so that their impact is less destructive. These might include art therapy, counseling, physical exercise, and writing out your feelings in a 'Grief Journal.'*

# Part Three

## Reflecting & Recreating

# The Waiting Room

## First Passenger

"Just go on without me, I'm not coming. I don't want to travel on with the rest of you. I can't travel on, because I belong here. This station is where I need to be. It's where my heart lies, my soul, my core, my 'reason to be.' For it is here I gain a sense that he hasn't gone. I feel he is with me in this place. He fills these four corners with his essence. If I stay, I won't feel so far from him. It will be as if he hasn't left. I'm okay here on this slatted bench. Sure, it's hard and uncomfortable, but strangely comforting, as well. Train travel has lost its appeal. Just leave me here; it's where I want to be. I won't move on for now, and maybe never at all."

## Second Passenger

"I was on the train when I heard the news. I just got out at the next station. I needed to rest, recover, and think it all through. I sat in the waiting room for many days with many trains zooming by. Over time, some staggering realizations dawned. It hit me that something extraordinary had occurred - he hadn't gone at all. He had, instead, been placed deep and securely in my heart. His heart was now within mine, meaning he could travel with me for the rest of my days - we would never be parted. A heart within a heart, making double love capacity; and that's not such a bad thing."

With this assured knowledge, Second Passenger stood up with a briefcase in hand, proud and tall, walked onto the platform, and waited as the next train came to a halt in front of her. She opened the doors and confidently stepped on board.

She smiled in appreciation of the new depth and richness she felt deep within, secure in the knowledge that from now on hers would be a shared journey - one belonging to her, and her 'passenger within.'

## Third Passenger

At the station, she waited and waited, watching many trains pass. Deep within, she felt the pain of her loss. She cried, yearned - let it all out. Many passengers delayed catching their trains, to sit with her in the waiting area. They listened, stroked her back, brought her food, offered her a shoulder to cry on. Third Passenger named this station's waiting room, 'The Honoring Room.' It was difficult, but she felt a compulsion to sit there day after day, while watching all the regular trains pull up, take on their eager passengers, and zoom off. This loss had to be acknowledged; his life had to be honored.

One knowing, kind soul gave her a writing journal. Third Passenger accepted it, holding it on her lap for many days. Then one morning, she felt an urge to peer inside. Gingerly, she opened it and began flicking through its crisp blank pages. Without thinking, she took up her pen and began to write.

There flowed a tremendous outpouring of words: words of pain, sadness, regret, and disbelief. She wrote day after day, into weeks, then months.

She had almost filled the book when, one day, she felt a stirring - something new was being sensed. The grief well deep inside her was beginning to run dry; she had poured so much out. A restlessness was coming over her. As she sat waiting, she began to glance up at the electronic destination boards, taking note of the trains that were due. She strained to see if there was some recognition of the place names.

Then one morning, she knew with certainty that a pivotal point had been reached - her grieving had been largely done - the pull of ongoing life, the moving train, was calling her. The loudspeaker's announcement, "Next train leaving in two minutes," rang clearly in her ears. With a quiet resolve, she stood unsteadily from where she had sat for many months, cradling her journal in her arms. She turned and, with great care, placed it on the bench seat, giving its cover a gentle farewell stroke. Bending down, she picked up her briefcase and strode towards the waiting train.

Once on board, she recognized old familiar faces and greeted them. They remarked, "It's been so long; you seem different." She nodded, "I am."

She glanced back for one last glimpse of the waiting room, knowing she was leaving a part of herself behind. Turning to face the direction of the now fast-moving train, she gazed through its windows at the beauty of the landscape and the distant horizon in view. This old familiar journey seemed so fresh and new - she was seeing it with new eyes - with new awareness. Everything appeared unchanged, but, at the same time, was uncannily different.

As the train rumbled on, she could hear a constant, soft murmuring, barely audible, in the background. She came to know it as the distant echo of the words of her writings. Though left far behind in the well-fingered journal now resting on the waiting room bench, the memory of those outpourings and their significance would remain a constant part of all her future journeys. A melancholic accompaniment - akin to the faint strains of a beautiful, rich cello; strains of deep, rounded notes of gold. Reluctantly welcomed, and forever present.

> **Task:** To respond to grief in your own way and to experience it fully. To be open to the development of new insights and awareness that may appear.

---

***Gentle Tip:*** *At some point in the grief journey, we have a choice as to how we react to our loss and how we will grieve. This choice has the capacity to significantly affect the decisions we will make in our life's continued journey.*

---

# THE GOLD PANNERS

YOU WILL FIND ME HARD at it at the crack of dawn, panning for gold. I stoop knee deep in the chilly, fast-flowing 'Creek of Time Gone By,' searching, searching. I stand at the creek's bend where the waters slow somewhat, squatting low, scooping up slush with my well-used gold pan. I slide my murky catch to and fro, scanning it, keenly, desperately.

My eyes are peeled, as my mind races. Never-ending questions fill my head to the rhythm of the slush, slush. How could this have happened? What more could I have done? Was she happy - sometimes? Did she have enough love? Where has she gone?

This self-interrogation, this panning, is endless. Memories flash by - the happy times, the sad, the difficult. These come with sound grabs, snatches of the spoken word - a few pure gems among them, 'absolute gold' to be stowed away forever in the vault of my mind. Others turn out to be disappointments, ugly lumps of pain with jagged points that cut deep, if handled the wrong way. They are in the mix, though, regrettable, but there, yes, always there.

My hands become calloused, grazed, and toughened with the labor of it. My heart, too, is pounding during this ordeal. When the jagged ones surface, I try to discard these worthless lumps of grit - reject them, let them go. What use can bad memories serve? They are tossed out along with the mud and slush. I won't let them cloud my mind; spoil the gems I've collected, dull their shine. But try as I might, some escape my screening; I can't block and discard them all, it seems. I am no longer in total control.

I look around me and see other panners stooping precariously on the creek's steep banks with aching backs. They scoop up as much slurry as possible, all at once. Impatient and fresh to the task, they pan up far too much to process at one time. They try to rush it; get it over with. They forget how much effort and focus are required. They fail, too, to have rest breaks and to feed themselves well. Out in the hot sun, they're exposed, hatless - copping it full on. Their children come dangerously close to the riverbank, pulling at their parents' legs - "Come and play, Dad, Mom. Have a break! Come see what I made." But they are not heeded. The relentless panners do not raise their heads - gold fever has them in its grip.

"Later, later," they cry to them.

We, the new panners, toil on. Our backs ache and our knees buckle with the strain of withstanding the relentless current of the fast-flowing creek - rushing onward, trying to drag us with it. But, stubborn to our cause, our heels, we dig in deeper. We will not be budged.

Sleep does not easily come even after an exhausting day's work. Sleep and I wrestle with each other every night. It never used to be like this. Now, when unable to sleep, I give up on it; declare my defeat. Rising from my bed well before dawn, I take up my lantern and rusty pan and return to the murky memory waters to pan some more. My mind begins once again to churn - slush, slush - questioning, searching.

Surely, one day I will have found all that I have been questing for. Surely, the sparkling nuggets of gold will eventually surface and be revealed to me so I can finally rest and lay my pan on the side of the bank. Surely one day my search for some answers will cease.

> **Task:** To learn from our grief. A common component of grieving is the questioning – often involving the search for meaning and what else could have been done.

**Gentle Tip:** *We question ourselves over and over, hoping for some answers. The 'hows,' the 'whys,' the 'what ifs,' the 'why didn't I's.' We want to find some reasons or some meaning in it all.*

*At times, we may have to resign ourselves to the fact that some answers may never be known.*

*We learn to treasure the good times shared, knowing they are 'pure gold,' priceless and irreplaceable. Unexpected gems can arise, becoming new insights to carry us forward.*

*Look for ways to distract yourself and take some time out. Grief work can be exhausting; it takes its toll. Don't forget your other family members, including the children, who will still need you. Bring them in, make time for them, help them grieve, too.*

---

# The Heart Strings

My heart is ensnared. It is held by a grip that can get tighter and tighter. It is squeezed at random, day or night. I never know when it's going to come on, and it hurts with a pain all of its own. So many emotions whip around me, binding me up. Strands of different colored coarse string, some thin, some thick, lashed firmly around my poor, trying-to-beat heart. Each color signifies a different emotion I feel. I picture them: pink for love and tenderness, mauve for sweet memories, red for anger, blue for sorrow and regret. And black, of course, the black for guilt and resentment. So many strings that bind.

No one knows. No one realizes my internal struggles. I have mastered the art of crying on the inside, never revealing my inner distress on my face.

'Fake it until you make it,' I was once told. Is that really the way? Faking it gets harder, though, as the pains come on without warning, without mercy.

Sometimes, I find myself in the grip of the black string of guilt, being pulled with such force I must stop whatever I'm doing, sit down quickly, and begin taking deep breaths to revive - survive. Two hours later, it might be the red string of anger that starts up, pulling and tugging, tightening its grip - so strong that I think my heart will be severed in two.

I am thankful for the lulls when they arrive. At least, during these reprieves, my heart has some chance to recover. Over time, and with great will, I develop some measure of control. I learn how to unravel many of these colored strands, loosen their grip. My mind, always busy, full of introspection and musings, becomes a tiny pair of thread-snippers working furiously, snip, snipping away - casting adrift spent surplus strands of emotion. Now finally able to be loosened, and shed.

*So, What's Grief Really Like?*

One day, as I sat on a park bench, glazed over and deep in thought, a wispy-haired old man with startlingly crystal-clear eyes wandered over and sat down beside me.

He turned and, looking at me, said, in a voice barely audible, "I see it in your eyes, my friend, you're hurt, deep inside. I've been where you are now. I know how bad the pains can grip. Listen, I want you to know that you will get through this. This unraveling business. It's deeply personal and unpredictable. Comes on at any time. But I'm sure you know this."

I nodded, amazed that he could see right through me.

"Well, there's no logic to it, see, no sequence at all," he continued. "In my case, well, I just dealt with each one of those heart tugs as I felt them. I felt each one fully, as hard as it was, acknowledged its presence, and tried to fathom its message. It takes a bucket of bravery to do it, son, but I was determined to release my heart from their relentless vice. I wanted to be able to enjoy life again. So, I tried to get a grip on my emotions, instead of them gripping me. At times, I thought my chest would burst with the anguish of it all. Sometimes, all those colored strings seemed to be pulling at once, truly torturous. They would pull me up, halt me in my tracks. I'd have to take some deep breaths, get some fresh air, splash my face with cool water, just to get a chance to rest up a bit. Over time, however, I began to relax, smile - yes, believe it or not, I could really smile again, and enjoy myself."

I listened to him, straining to catch the wisdom in his whisperings. I asked him if all my strings would eventually unravel and fall away to set my heart free. He nodded slowly and replied, "Ah, yes, everyone wants to know that. They all want to be as they once were - pretend it hasn't happened. But this can never be so, I'm afraid. Most people's hearts are left a little entwined, permanently it would seem. Often with a few final stubborn strands of particular colors - different ones for everyone, but not always.

Oftentimes, it's the strand for longing or sorrow that is a common one that stays - but guilt, fear, and anger often stick fast too."

I looked up into his knowing eyes and asked, "Can you tell me which ones I'll have trouble unraveling and cutting free?"

He shook his head, "No, my friend, that I cannot do. That is for you to know, not me. We must each discover our own resistant strands through the unraveling process. It takes a great deal of work and time. You'll find, too, that your 'stubborn strings' will be pulled at odd times throughout the remainder of your life when 'tug triggers' appear."

He explained how 'tug triggers' can come in many forms: maybe the sound of a special piece of music, the taste of a certain food, a particular scent, the shape of a stranger's head, or visiting a special place. At these times, he explained, you feel unique pains - grief pains, dull and deep. These tugs on your heart can be so strong.

"But listen up son, although these tugs can be intense, they will be bearable pains. You will learn over time, as I have done, that they will not destroy you and that you will be able to live with them. In fact, these painful tugs on your permanent heartstrings may well become a constant reminder to you of the significance of the great love you feel for your loved one, and always will."

With these last comforting words, he gave me a final reassuring look, slowly stood, pausing to gently rest his frail hand on my shoulder, then shuffled away.

I sat on that bench for quite some time afterwards, not wanting to move. A new confidence was now brewing; I did not feel so defeated - if I did the work, the painful grip on my heart would eventually ease. I made a promise to myself that I would work it out - untangle and shed as many strings as I could. I also vowed to accept and learn to live with the stubborn ones that refuse to budge. I'd find some way to manage my pains when the strings squeezed tightly. I could survive this after all.

I sat there for a long time, minutes, maybe hours, just letting the gift of his wise words sink in - sink deep into the heart of me.

> **Task:** To learn about yourself and the emotions you harbor. To know that you can work through many of them and let them go - easing your grief burden. There is grief work to be done.

***Gentle Tip:** Don't hold your emotions in. Acknowledge them, all of them - helping them to unravel. There are many ways to express your feelings to mark your loss: Talk, write, draw, move, paint, cry, laugh, curse, thump a mattress, seek counseling, compose, create, build, ritualize, plant a shrub, make a pilgrimage, carve a candle, share, create and hold some post-funeral memorials, remember out loud, make a toast, throw a party in their honor, start a foundation, devote some time to a fitting cause, write a* *letter to your loved one in a card on each of their future birthdays or anniversaries.*

# Rowing to the Isle of Loss

Here I sit on the warm, soft sand listening to the soothing lap, lap of the gentle rhythm of the waves. They caress, soothe, and calm each of my raw senses. I respond fully to their every welcome stroke. I hear the cry of free-larking gulls swooping overhead - their call, a homecoming song to me. I taste the tang of salt crystals left upon my lips by the cool, nurturing breezes fresh in from the sea. I run my fingers through the sparkling grains of golden sand, letting them pour freely.

Over and over, I recreate my tiny, sandy waterfall. Over and over, I watch the grains of gold slip through my fingers - as I think of you.

I am deliciously alone on this Isle of Loss. I admire the wondrous twists and curves of driftwood strewn along the smooth shore; a barren scene, I concede, but strangely beautiful and comforting nonetheless, for it is here I connect with you. As I lie in the calm, azure shallows, I allow myself to remember - and the tears begin to stream. It is here I feel fully the immensity of my loss.

On this isle, I stay as long as I please, as long as I'm able. My trusty rowboat, with oars at the ready, waits on the sand for the moment when I decide it is time to head back, back to the mainland and the busyness of life with all its demands: role-driven and duty-bound.

Each time I make this journey to my private 'Isle of Loss,' I always leave something of myself behind: words of love or regret spoken aloud on the breeze, words I never had the time to express. Or perhaps make a promise I want to share with you. Whatever it is, I always know I feel lighter, a little more restored after my island stays. I have given something over and reconnected with you.

I venture back with a greater sense of understanding and incorporate this into a new way of being. I take back with me small treasures: a beautiful shell, a curved twist of driftwood, a sweet dried anemone - keepsakes to treasure and hold fast my memory of you.

I have no idea how often these visits will be or how long they will last - I guess I'll know when that time comes. But for now, I will make these trips 'to and fro' when I feel 'the pull' - and savor their every golden moment.

> **Task:** To permit yourself to grieve fully. To learn to sit with grief and not push it away. Also, to experience the transition between feeling the loss and learning to adapt to living in your 'new normal' life. This includes living in the 'now,' and making future plans.

***Gentle Tip:*** *Grieving involves oscillating between the field of loss and the field of 'the new.' Constant trips 'to and fro' will be undertaken. Given time, you may find you are spending less time on the 'Isle of Loss' and more on the 'mainland' - the place of your new normal and the future.\* You may also like to take some 'time out' from both of these; pull in the oars and rest.*

\*The dual process model of grief involves a dynamic oscillation between feeling the loss on the one hand, and adapting to post-loss life, on the other. This model of grief is proposed by psychologists Margaret Stroebe and Henk Schut (1999).

# THE LAVA POOL

THE TRANSFORMATION BEGINS. MY ENTIRE system changes state, from solid to liquid. I am a fluid mass, a seeming conglomerate of a thousand emotions. I froth, ferment, bubble. I become a foreign brew - a brew now activated with a life of its own.

At first, my bubbling is furious, red hot, and unpredictable. I warn others not to come too near for fear they will be scalded and maimed by my sudden eruptions. Geysers of pain can shoot up and through me without warning. These new inner forces frighten me. I become unknown to myself, now a boiling, frothing lava pool, filled to the brim with a multitude of emotions - fear, anger, sorrow, regret, guilt, hatred, resentment - they go on. The heat bubbles rise constantly, even into the chill of the night.

The outside world and the goings-on around me mean nothing, nothing at all. I am not in tune with any of it; the seasons pass unnoticed. I create my own pulse - have my own furnace. I am totally absorbed in my process, in what I am becoming. My sole purpose is to process, release, process, release. And so, the bubbles rise, they pop with seeming defiance - spasmodically, incessantly.

Friends and family stand around, wary, not understanding what is happening, what to do. They chew their fists and shake their heads, step forward, then hurriedly back. They crowd at the edge, worrying about this gurgling pool of hot-red that heaves and puffs. Clouds of steam rise, sometimes foul-smelling and smoky grey, other times rosy pink in surprising sweetness.

There is no rhythm - no pattern to the workings of this. An onlooker is heard to say, "This pool is like a special potion - never been brewed before, though I have known many like it. It can take ages. We won't know how it will end up till most of the heat comes out of it."

Over time, my bubbling becomes less furious. Periods of calm arrive. It looks like all my gurgling, my fermenting, is done. Months, maybe years, can pass with no activity. Then, out of the blue, yet another heat bubble gushes up. It may vent and explode with an angry bang or linger, over a period of time, popping gently, causing minor ripples that eventually peter out.

I am greatly changed. I have become a thick, bubbling pool of molten lava fuelled by an energy sourced and held deep within - within the core of me.

> Task: To accept that grief is not something we 'get over.' To prepare yourself for unexpected eruptions of grief emotions, even after much time has passed. Your grief may never become 'completely cold.'

***Gentle Tip:*** *Grieving is a long-term process. After a period of time, we may think it is complete - the emotions having lost much of their heat, their intensity.*

*This may largely be so, but some emotions may continue to rise to the surface intermittently for a time yet - perhaps, for the rest of our lives, and often 'out of the blue.'*

*Seek out your own way to deal with these; perhaps deep breathing, sharing with a trusted other, writing in a personal grief journal, seeking rest and solitude, time in nature, attending to your spiritual needs, if that is important to you.*

# The Cloak of Feathers

I HAVE MADE MYSELF A CLOAK. A special cloak of feathers. It will be worn every day, no matter the weather. I have stitched each feather in place with my own hand. Each feather represents an element of guilt I feel belongs to me. As I lift this heavy cloak from its hanger and lower it over my straining shoulders, the weight of it astounds. The feathers themselves are delicate and light, but there are so many of them.

I drape myself fully in this garment of penance each morning, choosing to wear it daily - for all to see. My shame and guilt, so clearly and rightly (I venture to say) in full public view. It is easy for me to get lost in its deep, thick folds - the 'old me' becoming almost unrecognizable. It drags on me, weighs me down, prevents me from rushing forward, hampers my style. Nevertheless, I keep telling myself this is how it should be - must be. This is how it's going to be from here on in.

Friends worry about me, saying I am punishing myself needlessly. They try to convince me to stop wearing it, or at the very least, say that my cloak's feathery layers need thinning out. To their mind, these multitudinous feathers of guilt do not apply. They tell me I'm being too hard on myself, too punitive. They claim I have designed a cloak that is just too heavy for anyone to bear.

"Cast it off, forget about it," they plead. For some reason, they think it is just that simple.

After listening to them go on and on about it, I decide to take some heed. I set upon a plan. I inform them that I will confer with Father Time, and together, it will be he and I who will decide.

This is our deal: 'If, after a period, Father Time and I concur that it seems right and fitting that a particular guilt feather should be shed, and, with only the gentlest of tugs, its stitching comes loose of its own accord, then I will agree to let it be cast off and drift away.'

I will stop myself if I feel the urge to rush and retrieve it in a bid to re-stitch it back in place. I will accept that it is time to let that one go - that it no longer applies.

As I sit on the edge of my bed, draped in my heavy cloak, preparing to face yet another day, I try to visualize how thick my feathered cloak might be in my future - perhaps on my final day. I wonder how many feathers there will be left, held fast in their place, just as they are today.

Clearly, Father Time and I have a lot of conferring to do between now and then. This 'thinning of the feathers' could take quite a while.

> **Task:** To examine our levels of guilt (a common, lasting grief reaction) and work through them, perhaps with some guidance, if they are too strong for you.

***Gentle Tip:*** *The 'if only' questions may arise constantly, leaving a sense of guilt when we cannot find answers that sit well with us. Go easy on yourself; self-blaming is a common grief emotion, as we often place fault at our own feet. Work through your questions, and, with time, when you are ready, you may be able to let some of them go. Be prepared to resign yourself to the fact that some answers may never come.*

# Caught in a Rip

Relaxing in the calm, azure waters of my beloved local beach - a glorious day with friends by the surf, when, suddenly, the terror hit. I was trapped in the grip of an almighty rip with an undercurrent so strong it took my breath away. Panicking, I began flaying about like a thing possessed, exhausting myself not knowing which way to turn - my strokes futile and hopeless. A constant battery of waves was swamping me, each one threatening to thump the life out of me. Drowning seemed a very real possibility. I could hear my friends, 'the land dwellers,' chatting amongst themselves on the sand, just a few meters away, laughing without a care in the world.

They coaxed, "Come, join us. Sit here on the towels. Time to hop out and eat something." How simple it should have been for me to take those few sure steps to mingle with them, enjoy myself, be one of them.

As they saw me swimming in the waves rolling in relentlessly, they would have no idea of my underwater struggles and the colossal effort it took to keep my head above water. I was like a duck paddling furiously below the surface, getting nowhere. How could they know, or not know, that I was trapped in an all-powerful backward pulling current - one from which I feared I might never escape. My arm waving had no effect - my cries, unacknowledged. Drowned out by the deafening surf, these signals were misinterpreted and ignored.

Then it came to me - to save myself, I had to stop fighting. Something within me had to change. A different stroke was needed here, one that understood the nature of this rip's force, one I could use to cut through it, stop me going under and being overtaken by its might. I had to talk to myself, seriously - tell myself to believe that I could, and surely would, find a way to swim with this, not against it. I had to accept my predicament and surrender to its lessons. Only then might I survive to be rejoined with the 'land-dwellers.'

After coming up for air following a real dumper, I noticed others swimming in the rip with me. Across the roaring surf, they called out, "Relax, man. Don't go so hard. You'll exhaust yourself and won't last the distance. You need to change your stroke. Swim more smoothly. Watch what we do. Lie on your back and rest sometimes. Follow us, we know this rip well. Done it before. We know how to cut across it."

With few other options, I decided to follow their lead and was eventually led out of the danger zone to safety.

As my feet touched the firm, familiar sand of the shore, I emerged from the ocean that day a new person - though no one would have known just by looking. I was a survivor of a long, arduous and fear-ridden experience, now greatly humbled and more aware of the risks and precariousness of the swim; the swim we call we life.

A new respect for the might, the depths, and the unpredictability of the ocean had grown. I had learnt how unexpectedly we swimmers could be 'dumped' then swamped by the fears that follow. Deep within, I was profoundly changed by my ordeal.

A new confidence had developed - I had pulled through. My struggles had strengthened some muscles, muscles I'd never known I possessed. Somehow, I felt stronger for my experience, not weaker.

"You're back, finally. Lunch is nearly over," my friends called out as they saw me making my way towards them, dripping wet and pulling bits of seaweed from my hair. "We thought we'd lost you to the call of the surf," they said.

"Not quite," I answered, as if to myself, "nearly, but not quite."

**Task:** To acknowledge the profound nature of your loss, and not deny it.

To make adjustments so that you can cope with your grief experience. Accept with certainty that this experience has the power to change you. Life, and you, will never be quite the same.

---

*Gentle Tip: From the outside looking in, it is difficult for others to understand your grief world and gain a sense of what you are going through. Try to help others understand how things are for you and how hard it can be. Learn not to resist grief. Paradoxically, its force can save you and 'deliver you back to shore.' Be receptive to adapting - learning some different strokes to deal with the grief waves when they hit. Try, too, to build your strength during the lulls in between - these grief waves never entirely cease. You may find you become a skilled 'grief wave-rider' as time goes by.*

# The Grotto Within

I AM HOLLOWED OUT. A CAVITY, dark and deep, has formed at my core, carved out by the whittling knife of grief. Chip, chipping away; day in, day out, it sculpts. When I attempt to speak, I hear my voice echo strangely, rebounding off its curved, newly formed walls. My voice now flat; my words muffled, lifeless. I decide I am not worth listening to. I clam up - withdraw. If I can't make sense of what I am saying, surely no one else will. I give up singing - my notes sounding so distorted as they bounce around the walls of my cavity within. Tunes become unrecognizable. They have no place. Song sheets are put away.

A part of me is now missing. Like a phantom limb, I feel a huge absence - or should I say presence. I am no longer whole. I harbor a large gash, a gaping wound inside. Hidden, granted, but there, very much there. It bleeds - the trickles ooze out. I feel them, dripping, deep within me. I sit at breakfast - drip, drip. At cafes - drip, drip. In meetings, in the cinema, at my desk - drip, drip, drip, drip. Then, after a time unmeasured by clocks, I feel the trickles mercifully begin to thin out; the flow starting to ease. A new membrane forms within, sealing most of the leaks. My haemorrhage now arrested; the faucet turned almost to 'off.'

The grief cavern within remains, however. This hole inside me, deep and real, mirrors the massive hole I feel in the larger world. I hear the constant phrase, 'Something is very wrong,' whispered over and over. I sense that a massive piece of life is missing - there is a hole in the universe. The very air itself feels strangely porous. I could push my hand through it into another realm. The world has an emptiness now, a barrenness, that will not go away. Nothing can ever be the same. My cavern within has become a fixture, a part of me. How can I carry this? How can I function with this huge emptiness I feel inside - and outside?

I sit with this for a long time seeking a solution - some way to carry this that will be more bearable. Then it comes - I decide to make it a special place of honor for him - a sacred tabernacle; a beautiful grotto within.

I set to work doing a little each day. I sandpaper its walls with love, then line them with gratitude - for my time spent with him. Luminous tiles are created, tiles of honor, painted with luscious golden swirls of appreciation. My grotto's enfolding walls begin to glisten and shine in their radiance.

I place a white candle at my inner grotto's centre. It emits a pure golden light radiating through me, giving me strength and fuelling hope. I feel its glow and warmth travel through my body, reaching to the tips of my fingers and the soles of my feet. This glow leads me - gives each day a purpose.

Tending my 'inner light' I now harbor has become part of my new daily ritual. Each morning, I sit in silence, close my eyes, go inward - calming, settling, soothing, honoring. At times, my inner light quivers. I strive to calm the inner winds of distress and pettiness which may be whipping menacingly around it. I feel a response - my light burns tall, bright, and strong.

A sense of wholeness is returning. I can now open my eyes wide to each new day with hope and expectation.

>  'The light of him, my son – my sun
>  sets within me
>  and together, at break of day
>  we rise.'

**Task:** To acknowledge your pain and nurture yourself as you begin to recover. When ready, ask yourself: Is there any way I can transform this into something positive and life-affirming?

It may be possible for your grief to become a fuel, powering you on.

---

**Gentle Tip:** *Be creative in your grieving. It can unlock and release your creative side, thus helping to propel you forward. Allow your loss to be acknowledged in a special, unique, and beautiful way. Your spiritual side may be stirred during this time.*

---

# Part Four

## Reacquainting & Renewal

# THE STRAY CAT

ON A DAY LIKE ANY other day, I opened my front door and a bedraggled stray cat sidled into my well-ordered, calm, and comfortable abode. It wanted a new home, and it had chosen mine.

"Out!" I ordered and heaved it with the broom towards the door. "You don't belong here. I hate cats, especially your type!" Grabbing it by the scruff of the neck, I tossed it out onto the street - where it belonged. The next day, I opened the door and there it was again, staring at me with its pleading, yellow eyes. Confoundedly, my 'curse and banishment procedure,' which I repeated day after day, seemed to be having little effect. For there it would be each morning - just waiting for me.

With my frustration at its limit, the next time it appeared, I picked it up, cursing it under my breath, marched to the end of the house, and shut it in the back room, where nobody goes. Settling down to have a snack and read the paper, I could faintly hear its pitiful, protesting cries. Clearly, it was not going to let up; it wanted to be released and be set free in my home; it wanted to be with me in all I did. These cries continued day and night. Each night was spent tossing and turning - its relentless pleas haunting me. They seemed to reverberate through every room in the house, and every cell of my body.

Then, a gloomy realization came over me. This despicable creature was not going anywhere. It was here to stay; it could not, and would not be silenced, shunned, dismissed or tossed out. Reluctantly, for the sake of some peace, and quite possibly my sanity, I stopped resisting it. The door was left open. I began to give this stranger some freedom to roam through my house, and a little of my time. I tossed it small morsels of food, occasionally stroked it, and, reluctantly, gave it a little attention. I even began to think of a name for it, this cat ever-present. I settled on 'Shadow Boy.' Fitting, I thought.

Over time, I found myself talking about Shadow Boy, more and more, sharing stories of him with others. He was so full of surprises. I told them about the way he would try to wake me each morning by pressing his paw into my cheek, or attempt to sit on my face, threatening to smother. I found myself quietly smiling at his tricks, but even so, knew him to be an infuriating creature, nonetheless.

I never quite knew when he was going to pounce, scratch, or attack me. Shadow Boy liked to lie quietly in a secret hiding spot, maybe under the bed or behind the curtains, then dart out at me as I whizzed past. Both his claws would dig deep into my skin, drawing blood, making me wail. These cursed scratches could take weeks to heal.

It was so hard to live with him at times, so hard I'd despair. His unpredictable ways could send me into a maelstrom of emotions: frustration, amusement, anger, sorrow, tenderness, all in the mix. I was constantly trying to find some sanctuary, some relief from him. I wanted somewhere to hide - no such place exists, I came to discover.

But then, to my surprise, I would occasionally summon Shadow Boy, allowing him to come close, let him rub against me, curl up beside me, soft and warm. I began to feel a connection to him. One morning, I looked at him sitting on the couch, snuggled in close, purring with such contentment, licking his paw, and cleaning his ears.

"Perhaps, Shadow Boy," I said, "I have finally managed to tame you after all."

Shadow Boy dropped his paw swiftly. He stared straight back at me with those all too familiar, all-knowing yellow eyes. "Or perhaps," his unblinking gaze told me, "I've managed to tame you."

He got me thinking. "Perhaps, my furry one," I whispered, "we have learnt to live in some kind of symbiosis together; learnt to be with each other in a way that might just possibly work, and last the distance."

> **Task:** Learning to acknowledge and accommodate this foreign feeling called grief, as difficult as that might seem.

***Gentle Tip:*** *Let grief in, don't shut it out. Get to know it, learn to 'be with it' - bit by bit, moods and all. You will be a long time together.*

# My Personal Pyramid

## Before the Topple

ALL WAS IN ORDER. I had graded my rocks over a long time, from base to apex. Each rock was strategically stacked and aligned in perfect pyramid form. I knew which ones were to be at the top, necessary, of great significance, vital to my purpose.

There were base rocks too, all of import, but none like those of my shining boulders poised on high in the greatest place of honor. It had taken me years to work out which rocks I valued the most.

I had finally decided and was now able to lay all of them in ascending order, from bottom to top, with confidence and certainty. I came to know my pyramid's structure well, having personally planned it and positioned each of the boulders into their rightful place.

My priorities were sure and set, just like the perfectly aligned and symmetrical pyramid before me. Its form, dependable and true, giving my life surety, purpose, and stability.

I felt rock solid.

## After the Topple

All is chaos. I scramble over the scattered pile of rocks, running my fingers over them, feeling their size and texture, trying desperately to recognize them. My fingers now blistered and worn, my legs cut, battered and bruised from crawling over this pile of rubble. I have a desperate need to rebuild my pyramid - without it, I don't know, and won't know who I am or how to be. I instinctively know, however, that it cannot be rebuilt as it once was. A new value system must be devised. My rocks need to be reordered, re-positioned, and re-prioritized. Past concerns, once given high value, may now need to be reassessed and perhaps pushed to a base position. In contrast, others, never before thought golden and vital to my existence, might now be deemed worthy of pride of place, the apex. There is much sorting to be done, lots to churn over, think through.

Like the pyramid, I feel collapsed, broken; the task ahead of me daunting. I am weakened by the shock of the fall. I seem to hurt myself every time I attempt to lift a boulder to carry it to its new place. It takes such effort.

Although this rebuilding process is going to take time - lots of time, patience, and strength - I remain resolute to see it through.

> **Task:** To reassess what is now important to you in life, and rebuild your value system.

***Gentle Tip:*** *Grieving is a time when we reflect on our values and priorities, and so come to know which of these we now hold most dear. The rating we give each of them may then lead us forward. Our newly realized priorities may guide us as we make future decisions concerning our* *continuing life's purpose. Grief can, for some, be a time of significant personal growth.*

---

# Pebble in the Shoe

Every morning, as I reach for my shoes, there is a small, hard pebble waiting there for me, just in one of them. Knowing this, I pick up the shoe daily, turn it upside down, and shake it as hard as I can. But, try as I might, this stubborn little stone will not, and cannot, be shaken out. Reluctantly, I step into it, knowing it will hurt like crazy - but what choice do I have?

Tears are never far away. I have devised different ways to walk with it, trying to make it easier for myself. Perhaps venturing only onto smoother path surfaces, or often changing the shoes I wear. Strangely, though, no matter which shoes I choose, I am constantly confronted by 'the pebble.' The pebble that will not be cast out.

I have things to do. The demands of daily life keep piling up; you can only plug a dam for so long! With a mountain of resentment, I decided that, somehow, I am going to have to find a way to walk well enough so I can perform these tasks, despite this compulsory cargo being on board with every movement.

This pebble makes its presence known to me every day, hurts like hell sometimes, an ever-present aggravation. Sometimes I get a shot of pain up my leg, firing through me like an electric current, zapping my every cell. It can happen anywhere, any time. Oftentimes, I have to hold fast, grip my fists tight, and just bear it, pretending nothing is happening, no matter where I am. And those around me are none the wiser as to what I am secretly dealing with.

I have to make compensations for it all the time: walk with a crutch, stand a little differently, lean to one side, slow my pace. Tucked well away deep within my shoe, nobody really knows it's there, unless they guess, or I tell them. They might notice, however, that I occasionally grimace, stumble, or curse – and find it difficult to keep up. They're puzzled by the new air of preoccupation I have about me. They say it's as though I am only half listening; that I'm not fully present. The other day, when I was out shopping with a friend, she commented that I seemed to need more rest breaks than I used to. I didn't let on; it was all too hard to explain.

I realized that if I let it, this pebble could become a real hindrance for me. It could make me think twice before doing anything, even the mundane, like checking the letter-box, walking to the clothes line. Such an effort to complete these simple tasks was needed. I wondered if it might leave me permanently disabled or completely immobile. This could not be. I had to find a way.

With time and sheer grit, I slowly became accustomed to the pebble's niggling presence and the shots of pain it caused me. I soon learnt that if I maneuvered the pebble in just the right position in my shoe, its presence could sometimes become almost unnoticeable. This allowed me to get on and do all I needed to: walk where I wanted, stand for as long as I liked. It seemed I did have some control over this after all.

I discovered something else, somewhat surprising, too. When acutely felt, this tough little bead could truly amaze by sending a surge through my entire system, not of pain, but of power: an energizing force. Its effect being unexpectedly motivating. When felt this way, it could energize me, spring me into action. I found I was able to jump higher, walk, and even run if I had a mind to, albeit in a completely different way.

An acceptance stance was eventually reached. To my great surprise, I came to view 'Little Peb' as a blessed curse, one under whose influence I would remain for the rest of my days - accepting the good and the bad of it.

> **Task:** Grief's presence makes itself known to you. Your challenge is to find a way to carry it that works for you.

***Gentle Tip:*** *Rest when you need to, pace yourself, and allow yourself lots of time to adjust. Tell others how far and how fast you can go; what you can and can't manage on any given day. Sometimes it is wise to hold things off until you feel stronger.*

*Allow also for the possibility of grief's potential motivational force. If this force arises for you, accept it willingly. Don't waste your grief; it has the potential to provide a force of energy that, if tapped into, can lead to surprising and remarkable outcomes. Post-traumatic growth can often be realized. For this reason, grief has been known by some as a gift, albeit one that is wrapped in black paper.*

# Release of the Dove

It has happened. It cannot be undone. It dawns; I cannot hold onto it any longer. The time has come to let it go. A familiar 'coo-coo' is heard nearby. Perhaps, it also senses its time is near. With a heavy heart, I walk across the room to unlatch the lock on the door of the golden cage - home to my treasured, pure white dove. The dove I have sung to, harbored, and nurtured for so many days. It has rewarded me with its contentment in being near me, its comforting calm, its unexpected gifts, and, more than anything, its love.

I reach in with both hands and gently wrap them around the soft, pure silkiness of its wings. No resistance is felt - this one is willing. No doubt it instinctively knows my intent. I walk to my old velvet armchair by the open window and sit with this wondrous creature held gently but securely in my enveloping hands. I feel the beat, beat of its little heart. I wish to fully savor these last moments.

I lift its warm body to rest against my cheek. I study its eyes, how deep and knowing they seem. I tenderly kiss the top of its head, feeling its softness, its warmth. A tear escapes from one of my eyes, and then the other. Why does this have to be? Everything was so rich, so perfect. Things will never be the same. I have wrestled with the thought of this impending day for so long; I can do it no more. It's time to set it free.

I know the pain of 'the release' will tear me apart. Somehow, I know too, though, that the timing is right, and that I have recovered - not entirely, but enough.

I gently stroke its perfectly aligned feathers from head to tail, over and over, whispering gentle words of gratitude and say that the time has come for us both to part but promise that my window will always be kept open, just a little, for it to fly in whenever it chooses, no matter what I may be doing at the time, or where I am.

Then I stand, cradling my grief dove with the gentlest of hands. Taking a final step towards the window, I place it carefully onto the sill. In silence, I watch it find its feet, fluff its feathers, and lift its head to gain its bearings. A rising needy panic deep inside me surfaces, and with it a sudden urge to snatch it back and hold it firmly against my chest - I want to hold it there forever, as close to my heart as is possible. But, with painful resignation, I stop myself and watch it inch closer to the sill's edge.

Then, with an effortless flash of its shining wings, it takes off and is suddenly soaring - circling over the gardens, the rooftops, the trees. I stand at the window transfixed by its smooth, confident motion. It is free, and in a strange but unsettling way, so am I.

I watch it for as long as I am able, but the power poles, the tall buildings, the chimneys, the antennas all get in the way. I stand on my toes straining to keep it in sight, but realize it is futile. It has flown.

Grudgingly, I turn and look back into the room. It's dull, cold, and empty. I faintly hear my name being called, as always, someone wants me. I look at the laundry basket brimming over with rumpled clothes to be folded. I feel the dog, with that imploring stare and leash in its mouth, thump its tail against my leg, walk time.

Before beginning to attend to all of these demands, I glance once more at the empty cage with the unlatched door, and then at the open window. Yes, it really has flown, it really is true - I am no longer bound.

I wonder, though, how long it will be before 'white dove' surprises me with a visit. I know, for sure, it will reappear, and, when it does, it will always be of its own accord, not mine, and more than likely, when I am least prepared for it.*

*The Continuing Bonds Theory (Klass, Silverman & Nickman 1996) proposes the importance of retaining a connection with lost loved ones, and developing a continued, though different, relationship with them.*

**Task:** To grieve fully, then acknowledge when your grief wound is sufficiently attended to, so that you may once again re-enter 'the flow of life.'

---

***Gentle Tip:*** *The intensity of your grief will lessen with time, though your grieving will never fully cease. Do not be afraid when its intensity dies down. You are not being disloyal when you begin to find joy and interest in life again. Be ready, when this occurs, to accept that this time has come, and 'let it go,' reassured in the knowledge that your love for your loved one will not be diminished. Your ongoing relationship bond will continue as you live out your future life.*

# THE INVISIBLE BACKPACK

I WEAR A BACKPACK. IT'S on my back all the time, though this is not evident to everyone. It can't be removed, and believe me, it is not for want of trying. The clasp holding the straps together is welded in a locked position. This pack is held fast. It weighs a ton, so crammed full of 'stuff.' Its weight feels unbearable to carry. It's as if a giant hand is pressing down on me so hard I can no longer straighten my spine. Its force prevents me from doing things the way I used to. This pack makes me stumble when I try to walk, it makes me want to lie down and not get up. It makes me weary all the time. Now that it's there, everything seems such an effort. I curse its need, its presence. I don't want to carry this lump of lead for the rest of my days. After months of this, my resentment grows. I tell myself, 'There has to be some way.'

I began experimenting with it. I discovered it helped if I held a friend's hand, finding it warm and comforting. By holding hands with a trusted other, perhaps a seasoned backpacker, I could be guided if I strayed; helped to stay on track. I discovered, too, that I could lean on them if my pack's weight unbalanced me. It even helped if someone just sat with me and listened while I lashed out about how tough it was carrying this oppressive load I was supposed to bear and bear.

As the months dragged by, I found myself exploring new ways to hold myself in an effort to carry it more easily. I wanted to get on and do all those ordinary things that seemed so effortless before: hanging out the washing, making the bed, playing with the kids, watching a movie, sharing a laugh with friends without discomfort, guilt, or distraction.

Time cranked past, and with it, slowly but surely, my spine, miraculously it would seem, began to straighten. I eventually stood taller and more erect. It seems I had always held some hidden reserves after all - stored deep within, ready to be drawn upon at times like this. Even though my gait had been forever changed, I was soon able to walk again with some fluidity.

I remember once, as I was heading out the front door, I caught a glimpse of myself in my hall mirror. I was struck by my own reflection. Where had my stoop gone? My shoulders looked square again; my back straight and strong. Testing myself, I found I was able to bend, stretch, leap, and even dance if I had a mind to. Sure, my style was different, but hey, what did that matter? I could live with this thing - I was doing it. I was proof.

I wondered how this was all possible with that cursed pack still on my back and being the same size it had always been; its mass unchanged. Then it hit me. I realized that it was I who had changed through all of this. The grief pack itself had remained unchanged. It was I who had been reshaped and reformed, being compelled to build some new muscle to accommodate my heavy load. It was I who had been altered and had grown through this ordeal. I had learnt to carry my grief - successfully. *

*Dr Lois Tonkin's 'Growing Around Grief' theory (1996) proposes that as time passes, a bereaved person doesn't shrink their grief but instead grows around it; forming new relationships, new experiences, living in a new way.*

**Task:** To learn to deal with the grief you are carrying, knowing it is you who will change for this to be achieved. To seek ways to build inner strength, so that you learn to carry your grief well.

**Gentle Tip:** *The 'weight of your grief' may lessen with time and some of your own processing. This, however, is not because the weight of your grief lessens, but because you discover ways to live with, and grow around your grief - you build new figurative muscles. New ways of living* *and interacting are developed as you carry your grief - though its size remains much the same as it always has been.*

---

# THE PEARL DIVER

**S**PLASH! My morning ritual begins. Off the pier I dive into the sparkling sea, yet again. It's early, fresh - and the rest of the world is just waking up. I leave my friends to busy-about with all they have to do, preferring to take this dive alone. They seem to be used to me being absent these days. My aim, to dive deep into the depths, for it is there that the secret lies.

I work up my courage each morning to take the plunge. It's a struggle; diving is something of which I have had no experience in the past. I'm told to be cautious by others who have been there before and know the risks. These waters are full of mystery. They say there are hidden caves, deep troughs, and sudden ledges. Deep down, it is dark and eerie; all is unknown to me. I feel my way in the darkness. What am I in for?

As I dive, deeper and deeper, with a mesh basket in hand, I experience the change in the water's temperature. I pass through warm patches, then into cold, these dives can be so unpredictable. You never really know what you might encounter. Sometimes, fear grabs hold of me, making me want to turn back instantly, stay where it is warm and familiar - be home. But I can't, my quest must continue. I stay brave, resolute, keep swimming further and further, deeper and deeper.

I dive until my breath begins to go. I test myself each time. As I near the bottom, I keenly scan the ocean floor for oyster shells to be gathered up and stowed in my basket. I work quickly; there is never enough time. When my lungs are strained to their limit, I turn to swim upward, trailing my haul to the surface and heaving it onto the wooden pier. Clambering up the ladder, I spread out my catch across the boards. With shucking knife in hand, I pry each oyster open - inspecting, examining, always hopeful. "What am I looking for?" I'm not really sure, but I know I will be when it is found. Is it peace? Reassurance? Forgiveness? An answer? A calling? A lesson? I want to find some meaning in all this.

I wonder with every dive, "Will today be the day when I will be gifted with my reward?" There must be a reason. There must be an end, eventually.

For months now, I have taken this daily dive into the depths. It's cold, lonely, and seemingly fruitless work. So many times, I have surfaced with 'worthless clams,' heavy and empty. I have wanted to give up, return to regular routines, be none the wiser.

But, no, there is a yearning deep within that drives me on - a real sense that there is something to be discovered in all of this. I am certain, to the core of me, that all of this cannot end in 'nothing,' be for nothing. I am sure that one day I will spread my haul to finally pry open that one special oyster that reveals the precious, gleaming pearl of wisdom in this loss, and claim it as mine.

**Task:** To keep exploring the seemingly unattainable possibility that there is some meaning to this loss. *

---

**Gentle Tip:** *Allow time for quiet reflection. Read inspirational literature that 'speaks to you;' poetry, philosophical and religious texts, whichever appeals. The meaning of life and how it is to be lived may be a common theme of new interest, as well as the meaning of loss and the possibility of an afterlife, or not. Grief can be a time of searching. Gifts of rich insights may surface for you.*

---

*\*The Grief Model of Constructivism, as proposed by Robert A Neimeyer (1993), stresses the importance of each individual's 'meaning-making' from the loss experience.*

# THE TAPESTRY WEAVER

I BELONG TO A LOCAL WEAVERS' GROUP. We meet weekly at the back of the town hall.

We're a lively, creative bunch, passionate about weaving, and we love to share our skills. We design and weave our tapestries, then proudly exhibit them. The last tapestry I created was going so well. Many admired it. "So beautifully woven, such vibrant colors, glowing with life and vitality," my fellow weavers praised.

I loved adding new colors to my wool basket, which I'd happily weave into my tapestry with love and care. Wondrous shades of bright yellows and oranges, brilliant pinks, radiant reds, and lively greens - all my favorites tossed in the mix. Each morning, I would rush through my chores, eager to begin my weaving. Weaving soothed me, it gave me such joy as I worked the shuttle to and fro. With each passing day, my efforts were rewarded. My wonderful, rich tapestry grew before me, filled with vibrant life-affirming swirls. I loved the joyous creativity of it. Life was good.

One morning, as I sat down to weave, I found a ball of blue wool in my basket. I had no idea how it got there - it was a color I never chose myself. "Never mind, no bother," I declared, "I just won't use it." Settling down by the open window, I began preparing my loom. I reached for a ball of pink, but as I lifted my hand, I was surprised to find it was not the cheery pink wool ball I was holding but a dull blue one.

I laughed at myself, thinking I must still be sleepy, and tossed it back in the basket. For the second time, I reached for the pink, but as I looked down, I was confounded to discover it was the ball of blue again that lay in my hand. Now I was getting angry. Blue had no place in my tapestry; it was dreary and melancholic. It would dampen the tone of my work. I threw it back in the basket, cursing it under my breath. This time, I carefully hovered my hand over the desired ball of pink, then dived for it.

It came up blue, again.

"This is unbelievable," I protested, stamping my foot. "What's going on here?" Try as I might to have only the bright colors of my choice, it was the blue wool each time I was landed with. Somehow, I concluded, I was being compelled to work with the blue. Was it being willed upon me? Defiantly, I declared blueness had no place. My tapestry's beautiful design would be ruined.

After many more unsuccessful attempts to reject the blue, with a heavy heart, I gave in. I resigned myself to the fact that, if, in order to keep weaving, I must include some blue in my design, then so be it - some blue there would have to be.

As I wove, I noticed, too, that the thickness of the blue yarn kept changing as it was unraveled. Some days the thread would appear thick and strong, highly noticeable, and other days it would be thin and faint, barely visible at all. But one fact was sure, 'the blue' was always there, each and every day.

I took my unfinished tapestry along to the hall to show the more experienced weavers. I wanted to share my struggles with them and seek some help. As I spread my tapestry on the wide central table, I glanced at all the other tapestries spread across it; I was stunned. For the first time, I became aware that every tapestry had some threads of blue woven into it - the same dull, melancholic blue as mine. I was looking with new eyes. Why hadn't I noticed this before?

Hillie, a much-loved long-time weaver, wandered over to me, and casting her sharp eyes over my piece, said, "Ah, I wondered when your time would come, my dear. The 'blueness' comes to us all, eventually. And when it does, we really do not have much say in it. Did you find that?" I nodded silently, completely stuck for words.

I thought I knew it all before now, but clearly, not so. I thought my design was totally in my control. I listened as she gently spoke, telling her story as she keenly scanned my piece with her expert eyes. "I started weaving with the blue forty years ago. Take a look around," she continued, turning to face the room. I glanced around at all the magnificent tapestries spread before me. As I did, I could see that each of these beautiful creations possessed an amazing richness and balance to them. Each held a real beauty and depth - and yet each was woven with some threads of 'the blue,'

I nodded again, slowly telling her, "I realize now, Hillie, my tapestry needed light and shade; warm colors, and cool. It just wasn't balanced before. The blue needs to be part of it - a good tapestry displays the full color spectrum. I think I get it now. We notice the pinks and yellows more because of the blues."

Hillie gave a gentle nod and replied, "That's it, you do understand. Learning to weave with the blue is something we will all learn to do, sooner or later. It changes the way you see everything. It's just that this time it is your turn - your time has come."

> **Task:** To learn to weave our grief into our individual life's tapestry in our own unique way, knowing it has a place and is a part of life. We learn to accept, as difficult as this can be, that death is part of life.

**Gentle Tip:** *Know that you are not alone as a griever. You are in good company. Seek out trusted 'weavers of blue.' Spend time with them: go for coffee, take walks together, listen, and share. Listen to their tips on how to manage grief, how to stitch in the 'bad times.' Let them be your guides to understanding that grief can bring about a new awareness, an awakening. Perhaps a heightened understanding may arise regarding the everyday human experiences of not only the joys of life, but also the sorrows. Your awareness of, and empathy for, other grievers may be strengthened considerably as well.*

# Metamorphosis

THE MOMENT I HEARD THE news, my world started to spin: my mind, my body, the walls, the floor, all tossed into a wild revolution. My greatest need was to escape, escape from this reality-shattering moment. I spun and spun the threads of it all until I was enfolded deep within a soft, dark, and wonderfully cavernous cocoon far from the bright, annoying lights and sounds of the world; all far too much for me now. I decided it was here I needed to stay. I could not face the world as I was. The 'one I was' had disintegrated, never to return. There I lay in my welcomed hideaway, brooding, ruminating, evaluating, pondering, chewing it over and over. I knew there would be no time limit to this metamorphosis; it would take as long as it demanded.

Others peered in, tried to pry me out. They prodded and coaxed, called my name. They brought their guitars, sang, and played joy-filled music they knew I loved in the hope of enticing me to reappear, smiling as I used to. They wanted to stir me into action, to no avail. I lay low, a still and silent fixture within, divorced from them, separate and alone. I now belonged to another time, another realm.

I lay cocooned within, for what seemed an eternity, until a change was felt. Deep inside, asleep and a little dream weary, I was awakened by a bright light shining in through a gap at the entrance. Its bright rays hit my face and flooded the inside of the cocoon with a warm, golden glow. Dawn was welcoming me.

I could hear the faint, sweet notes of a lone flute being played nearby, so clear and inviting. I began to move, surprising myself that I still knew how. Inching towards the aperture, I ruptured fully the casing of my cocooned world. Friendly, familiar faces greeted me, so encouraging, so happy to have me back.

## So, What's Grief Really Like?

I emerged, carefully unfolding my new self, body part by body part, then daring to unfold my moist, newly formed, colored wings. Something new and energizing was being pumped through my veins. My wings expanded of their own accord, and were now entirely on display - broad, powerful, and, though foreign to me, truly exquisite. With amazement, I realized the world had been carrying on all the while during my 'incubation.' I wondered how this could have been. How could things have changed so little when I, to my very core, had changed so much?

I moved among my old friends, thanking them for their welcome, their time spent 'watching over me.' It was lovely to be with them again. However, unbeknownst to them, I held deep within a new passion, planted and germinated during my metamorphosis. A new purpose swelled in my chest, and its fulfillment became my sole focus.

My only intent now was to find the perfect place, a place with some elevation with a clear expansive view. In my new guise, I moved about in the hustle and bustle of life, reacquainting myself with it. All the while, however, my eyes were peeled, trying to find my longed-for 'launching place.' After a time, a 'knowingness' came over me; it was found - a steep, craggy cliff ledge poised high above a broad and luscious valley.

There was a 'rightness' to all of this. There would be no turning back. I moved to the edge of the ledge, paused a while, gathering my strength and all the courage I could muster. Turning, I smiled at my friends and family, who, though full of doubt and disbelief, had come to bear witness. Resolutely, I faced forward.

Balancing myself on the cliff's edge, I surveyed the vast view stretching before me. Focusing my energies, I allowed my powerful, broad wings to slowly unfold and spread fully in all their glory. The surrounding grasses and trees seemed to bow in unison, in approval. As my heart swelled with a new confidence, I leaped.

Upon the passing of the next mountain breeze, I lifted - rising without a sound and majestically took flight.

> **Task:** To do the grief work and be prepared for any transformative possibilities that may appear for you.

---

**Gentle Tip:** *Grief cannot be rushed. Give it all the time you feel you need. You may emerge from this with a new sense of purpose or perspective. New goals may appear. You may decide it is time to change tack; the old ways may no longer seem applicable to your 'new normal' life, though this is not always the case. After thinking it through, do what feels right for you. Go with it and live it out, your way.*

---

# Acknowledgements

Some years ago, this book was but a seed of an idea.

I am most grateful to those friends and colleagues who encouraged me to believe in the concept of a collection of personal reflections as a helpful way to illuminate the many facets of the grief experience.

I would especially like to express my gratitude to my valiant son, Carl, whose life is honored within these pages - he remains a constant inspiration to me. I remain forever grateful for the honor he gave me of being his mother. His loss, such a profound life-altering event, pierced a creative bubble deep within. The transformative nature of the grief I experienced left me with a genuine need to express. This collection is its culmination.

I would also like to thank my siblings and extended family members, whose great sensitivity and support helped me enormously, both in my grief, and to see this project through to its completion.

My sincere gratitude to Richard Harrison, of Fairlawne Publishing, for his great interest, thoughtfulness, and consideration throughout the publishing process. To Peter Deerson, also, for his invaluable encouragement and help with my manuscript.

Lastly, I would like to thank the many grievers who shared their often raw and painful grief experiences, individually felt; their heart pains, their desperations, their yearnings, as well as their sweet memories. The strength and authenticity demonstrated in their willingness to 'tell it like it really is' was truly astounding. Their 'revelations' feature strongly among this book's pages and are embedded in many of the reflections described.

*So, What's Grief Really Like?*

This book pays homage to them, and to all grievers, of all kinds.

# NOTES

www.ingramcontent.com/pod-product-compliance
Lightning Source LLC
Chambersburg PA
CBHW070044230426
43661CB00005B/753